My more-than-coloring book about

Easter

Cathy Spieler

Illustrated by Ed Koehler

Cover illustrations by Steve Sauer,

with help from Kayla Lohman

CPH
SAINT LOUIS

Thank you to the children at Christ Community Lutheran School in St. Louis, MO, who worked hard to give us pictures to choose from for the cover of this book. Each picture was delightful and creative!

A More-than-Coloring Note to Adults

This activity book is more than a coloring book where children simply fill in someone's line drawings with color. Because children have their own ideas about how things should look, this book is written in such a manner as to spark ideas and invite children to use their imagination and creativity to complete each picture.

There is no right or wrong way to finish each page. Crayons or markers can easily be used to finish the pages or, if children wish, scraps of paper, glitter, or other available materials can be added to enhance each creation.

A More-than-Coloring Note for Children

The pages in this book are not finished. They are waiting for your great ideas and artistic creativity to make them complete.

Have someone read the words on each page to you or read them yourself. Then think about your ideas and decide how you would finish the picture.

God has given you great gifts and abilities. It's your turn to use them to make your own more-than-coloring masterpiece!

Jesus rode into Jerusalem. The people cheered and laid coats and branches from trees on the road. Draw the road. Add some coats and tree branches.

Children came to the temple and sang praises to Jesus. Draw the children. Would they be dressed the same way you dress?

Jesus ate the Passover meal with His friends, the disciples. Draw some of the disciples next to Jesus.

Jesus prayed to God the Father in a garden called
Gethsemane. You see Jesus, but there are no plants or trees.
Draw plants and trees in the garden.

Jesus was arrested and taken before the high priest. Draw Caiaphas, the high priest. What kind of clothing would he be wearing? Would it be fancy or plain?

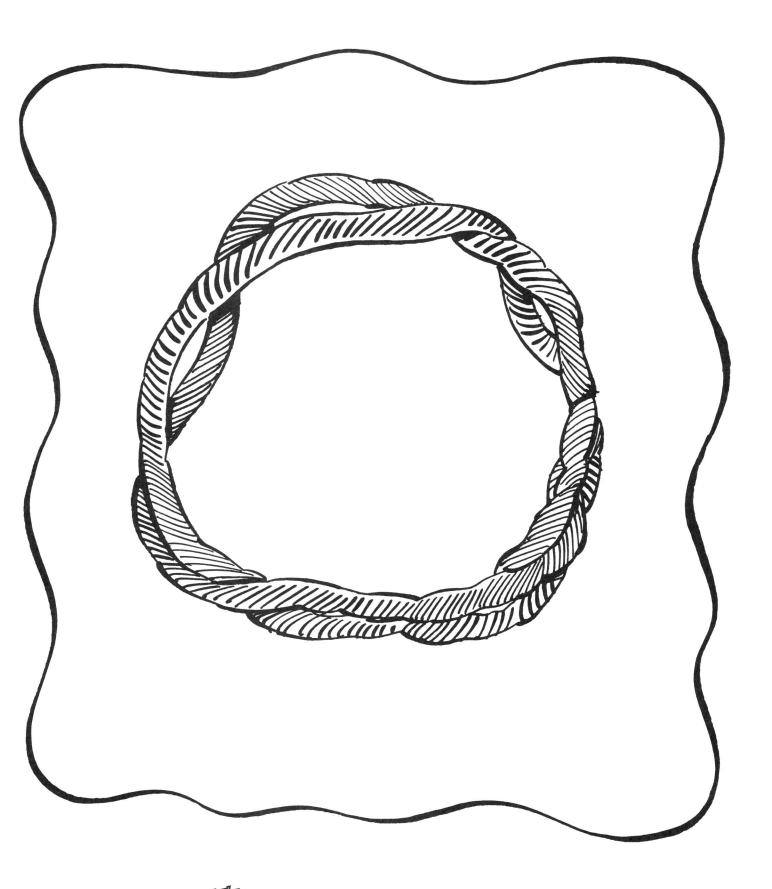

The soldiers made fun of Jesus.
They placed a crown of thorns on His head.
Draw some prickly, stickly thorns on this crown of thorns.

A man named Simon carried the cross for Jesus. Draw the cross Simon is carrying. Add more people to the crowd. How do you think the people felt?

Jesus was crucified on a cross between two criminals.
Draw the cross for Jesus in the middle.

After Jesus was buried in the tomb, a guard stood outside to make sure that no one would steal the body. Draw the guard standing watch.

Jesus did not stay dead. He rose again on Easter.
There was an earthquake and the stone was rolled away.
Friends of Jesus saw an angel. Draw the angel by the tomb.

23

Before Jesus went back up to heaven, He told the disciples to tell others all about Him. We can tell others the Good News of His love too.

Even though Jesus is in heaven, He is always with us because He loves us. Draw a picture of Jesus to help you remember that He is always with you.

Sunrise services are often held on Easter.
The rising of the sun shows that a new day is beginning.
On Easter we know that we have New Life in Jesus.
Color a beautiful sunrise on this page.
Use yellow and orange to make it bright.

Eggs are a symbol of New Life. We decorate Easter eggs with colors and designs to celebrate the New Life we have in Jesus. Decorate these eggs with beautiful colors and shapes.

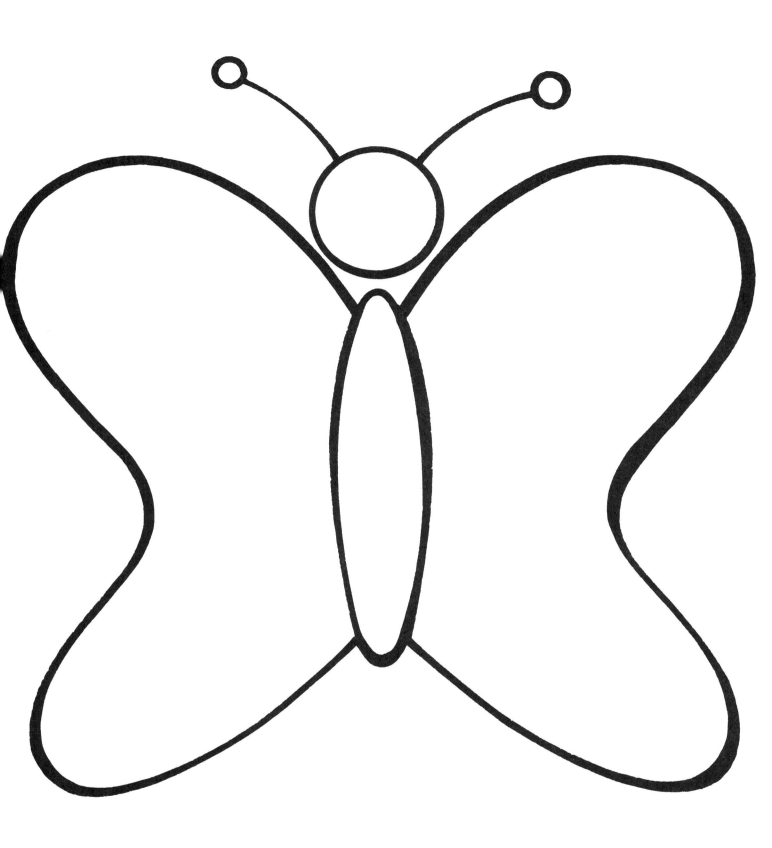

The butterfly can also be a symbol of New Life in Jesus.
Decorate this butterfly using lots of the beautiful colors
God has made.

God made caterpillars so that they will change into something very beautiful. Draw a caterpillar crawling on the tree branch.

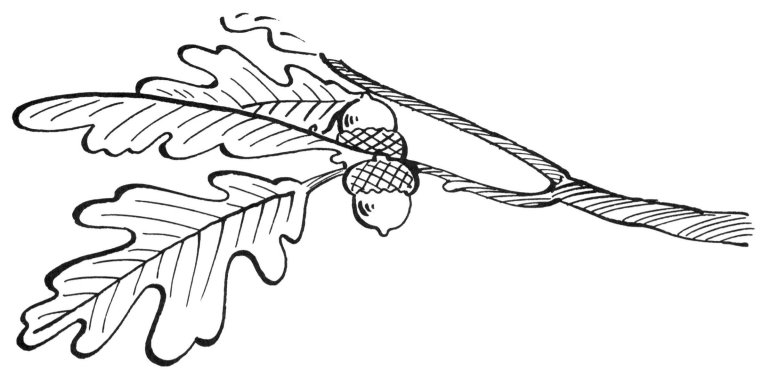

Caterpillars eat and eat until God tells them it is time for a change. Then they hang upside down and cover themselves with a chrysalis. After several weeks they change into butterflies. Draw a chrysalis hanging from this tree branch.

Butterflies come out of a chrysalis.
Jesus came out of the tomb.
Draw lots of beautiful butterflies on this page.

In the spring, birds build nests and lay eggs in them.
Draw some eggs in this nest.

41

Baby birds will hatch out of the eggs.
Jesus came out of the tomb.
Draw the baby birds that have hatched from the eggs.

Baby bunnies can also remind us of our New Life in Jesus.
This mother rabbit is looking for her baby bunnies.
Draw her baby bunnies on this page. Where are they hiding?

Baby ducks can also remind us of our New Life in Jesus. The mother duck is swimming and leading her ducklings. Draw some baby ducklings behind the mother duck.

New clothes can also remind us of our New Life in Jesus.
Do you get a new outfit for Easter? Draw a picture of an outfit
you might wear to church on Easter Sunday.

Sometimes people wear pretty hats at Easter. Add some flowers, ribbons, or other decorations to make this a special Easter bonnet.

We often get together with loved ones and eat special foods to celebrate Easter. Draw the food you would like your family to eat at Easter.

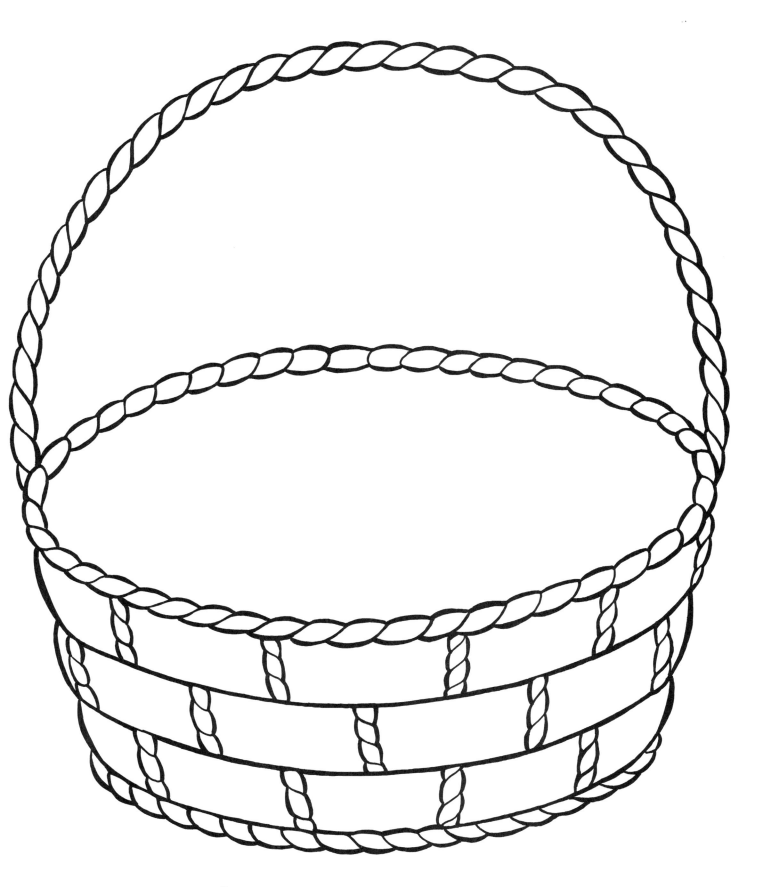

Easter baskets full of treats are another way to celebrate at Easter. This basket is empty. Fill this basket with things that would make you happy at Easter.

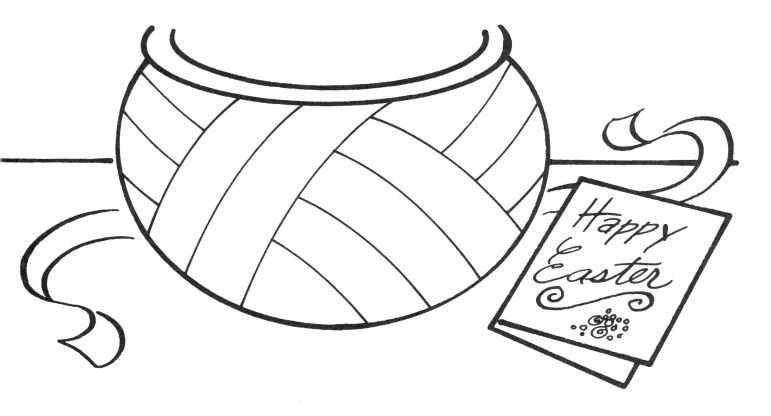

Easter lilies are often used in churches to decorate for Easter. Draw some Easter lilies or other flowers in this pot.

We decorate the front of our churches for Easter with flowers and palms. Decorate the front of this church so that it will be ready for Easter.

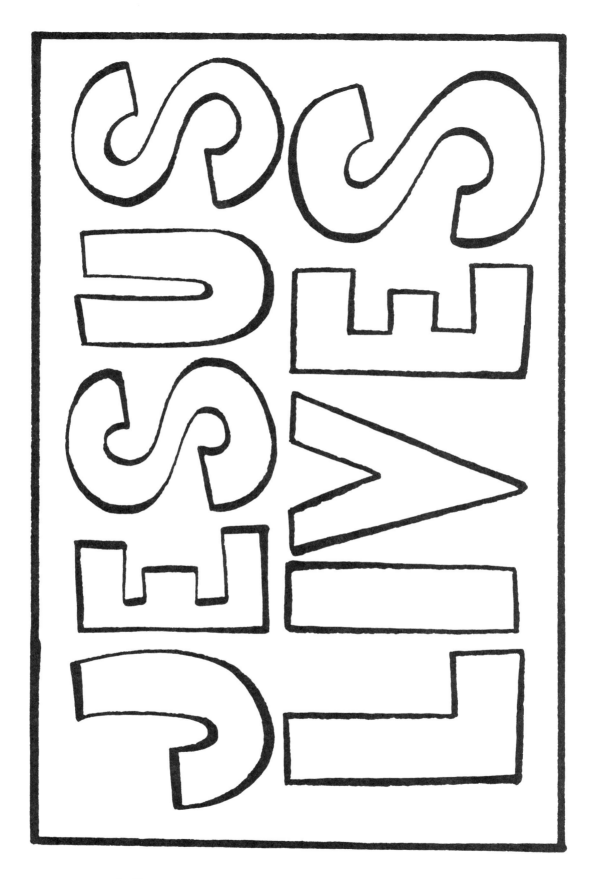

We would like the world to know that Jesus lives.
Add bright colors and decorations to this sign
to let everyone know that Jesus is alive.

We are happy when we hear the Good News story of Jesus'
resurrection. Draw a picture of you in your finest Easter clothes.
Show that you are happy that Jesus is your Savior.

The End